SPOT and STICK

Robin Kerrod

Illustrated by
Tim Hayward

Purnell

Contents

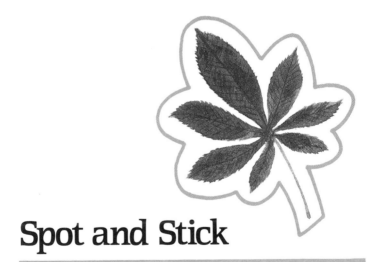

Spot and Stick

You will notice in the book that some of the trees have a star next to their names. This tells you that there are stickers for these trees. When you spot one, cut out the sticker and stick it in a suitable place on the frieze. You can either leave the frieze at the back of the book, or you can cut it out and stick it on the wall.

Trees

Editor: Janine Amos
Designer: Ruth Hall

ISBN 0 361 06676 7

Copyright © 1985 Purnell Publishers Limited
Published 1985 by Purnell Books, Paulton, Bristol BS18 5LQ
a member of the BPCC Group
Made and printed in Great Britain by Purnell
and Sons (Book Production) Limited, Paulton, Bristol
Phototypeset by Quadraset Limited

Introduction

Trees are the biggest plants on Earth. Some fir trees in Britain grow up to 55 metres tall. Trees also live longer than any other plants. Some yews in Britain are thought to be up to 2000 years old.

The yew is a tree which has leaves like needles. So do the Scots pine and the juniper. These are the only needle-leaved trees that are native to Britain— that came from here originally. Most of the trees you see in the countryside have broad leaves. There are 32 kinds of broad-leaved trees that are native to Britain, including the ash, oak, lime and willow.

Over the years many other kinds of trees have been brought to Britain, and over 1000 different kinds now grow here. But only about 150 of them are common. Many of the introduced trees are grown in man-made forests for their timber.

Using this Book

In this book we have divided up the trees according to the shape of their leaves. Round and oval leaves; leaves with lobes; long leaves; compound leaves; needle-like leaves; and scaly leaves. You can see examples of these kinds of leaves on page 5.

When you spot a tree you want to identify, look at its general shape, and examine its leaves and any flowers, seeds and fruits. Then try to match these features with pictures in the book. Look in the section covering the kinds of leaves the tree has. The text gives more information to help you identify the tree.

The main tree names given in this book are the common names. Underneath are the scientific names, given in Latin. The first part of the Latin name gives the genus of the tree. This is the name of a group of similar trees. The second part of the Latin name gives the species of the tree. This refers to one particular kind of tree within the group.

Crack willow

English oak

Pollarded Crown

Broad Crown

Weeping willow

Lawson cypress

Weeping Crown

Triangular Crown

Tree Shapes

Left by itself, a tree will eventually grow into a certain shape. The shape is formed from the trunk and the crown. The crown is the mass of branches, twigs and leaves.

In general broad-leaved trees have a much broader crown than needle-leaved trees. The broad-leaved oak has a broad, rounded crown. The crown of the needle-leaved Lawson cypress is broad at the bottom, but narrows gradually to a point at the top, like a triangle.

The picture above also shows two other interesting shapes. The weeping willow has a weeping crown. Its thin branches hang down rather like water cascading over a waterfall. The crack willow has been pollarded, or cut off to allow thin branches to grow.

4

Tree Leaves

It is often difficult to recognize a tree by its shape alone. A better way is by looking at its leaves. Leaves come in a number of basic shapes, and this gives us a way of dividing trees into six groups.

The pictures below show examples of the kinds of leaves in each group. Lobed leaves have very wavy or cut-out edges. Compound leaves are made up of small leaflets.

Round and Oval Leaves

Hornbeam

Aspen

Lime

Lobed Leaves

English oak

Long Leaves

Maple

Willow

Compound Leaves

Needle-like Leaves

Silver fir

Scaly Leaves

Ash

Lawson cypress

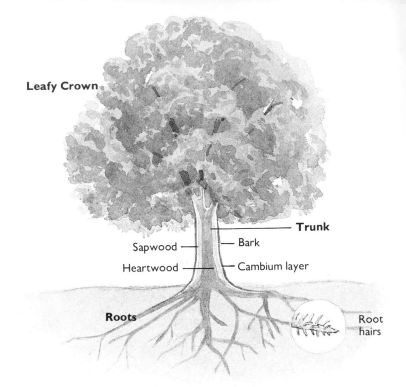

Leafy Crown

Trunk

Sapwood — — Bark

Heartwood — — Cambium layer

Roots — Root hairs

The Living Tree

The main parts of a tree are the roots, the trunk and the crown. The roots have two main jobs. They take in water from the soil through tiny hairs. They also act as an anchor to stop the tree blowing over.

The trunk is made up mainly of wood. It provides the strength to support the leafy crown. The bark on the outside helps protect it. The water taken in by the roots travels up the trunk to the leaves. It travels through 'pipes' in the outer wood, called sapwood.

Between the sapwood and the bark is a thin layer called the cambium. This layer grows outwards and builds a new ring of wood each year.

The job of the green leaves in the crown is to make sugar as food for the tree. They make the sugar using water (from the roots) and carbon dioxide gas (from the air).

Most trees with broad leaves drop their leaves in the autumn. We call them deciduous trees. Most trees with needle-like and scaly leaves keep their leaves throughout the year. They are evergreen. Most of them carry their seeds in woody cones. We call them conifers.

Tree Buds

Every spring the new growth of a tree starts at the buds on the twigs. New leaves grow from the side buds. New shoots grow from the terminal (end) buds. By the autumn new buds have formed.

In time you will be able to recognize many trees just by their buds, because every kind of tree has different buds. Some are shown below. Notice also that the buds can grow in different positions along the twigs.

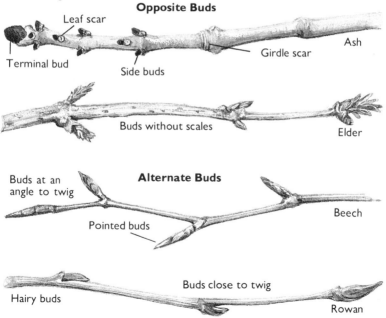

Opposite Buds

Leaf scar

Terminal bud

Side buds

Girdle scar

Ash

Buds without scales

Elder

Alternate Buds

Buds at an angle to twig

Pointed buds

Beech

Buds close to twig

Hairy buds

Rowan

Round or Oval Leaves

Aspen
Populus tremula

Height: 20 metres

The leaves of this small tree rustle in the slightest breeze. In autumn they turn bright yellow. The bark is silvery in colour.

★
Common Alder
Alnus glutinosa

Height: 22 metres

The alder loves wet ground. You usually see it along river banks. The fruits are like tiny fir cones and stay on the tree all winter.

Hornbeam
Carpinus betulus
Height: 24 metres

This tree is often found in oak and beech woods. The leaves are rougher than beech leaves. The fruits are called nutlets, and they grow in clusters inside long 'leaves'. The wood of the hornbeam is very hard and tough.

★

Goat Willow
Salix caprea
Height: 15 metres

This tree is also called sallow and pussy willow. The goat willow loves wet ground, like all willows. You often see it near water. It is called pussy willow because the fluffy catkins look like a cat's fur.

9

Common Beech
Fagus sylvatica
Height: 36 metres

The beech has wide,
spreading branches and
smooth grey bark. Beech
woods are shady places
because the sunlight
cannot get through the
leaves. In autumn the
shiny green leaves turn a
beautiful orange-brown
colour. The copper beech
is a variety of beech with
reddish-purple leaves.

English Elm
Ulmus procera
Height: 36 metres

Once you could see these
elms almost everywhere in
the English countryside.
But now many have been
killed by Dutch elm
disease. The seeds of the
elm are like little wafers.
They are green at first,
then they turn brown and
fall in the summer.

Smooth-leaved Elm
Ulmus carpinifolia
Height: 27 metres

This is the common elm on the mainland of Europe. Its leaves are bright green, shiny and smooth. The bark of the tree has deep cracks in it—much deeper than those in other elms.

Wych Elm
Ulmus glabra
Height: 30 metres

You often find the wych elm near water. Its leaves are more pointed than those of the English elm, and it also has more spreading branches. In autumn the leaves turn golden yellow.

Common Lime

Tilia × europaea

Height: 40 metres

The flowers of the common lime have a powerful scent and attract bees in early summer. The flowers, and later the fruits, grow from a pale green 'wing'.

★
Wayfaring Tree

Viburnum lantana

Height: 6 metres

This small tree produces thick heads of white flowers in spring. The green berries that follow turn first red and then black as they ripen. Notice that the leaves grow opposite one another, in pairs.

Large-leaved Lime
Tilia platyphyllos

Height: 30 metres

Like the other limes, the large-leaved variety has leaves shaped like a heart. Its flowers come out before those of the other limes and are much bigger.

Whitebeam
Sorbus aria

Height: 24 metres

Notice the silvery underside of the leaves of this tree. They are covered in thick hairs. Look for the heads of creamy white flowers, which appear in May and have a sweet scent. The berries that form turn bright red in the autumn.

Silver Birch
Betula pendula
Height: 30 metres

You can recognize this tree by its silvery-white bark. The tree is tall and slender, and the branches are thin and droop at the ends. The leaves turn yellow in the autumn.

Downy Birch
Betula pubescens
Height: 24 metres

The downy birch grows in wetter places than the silver birch. It is broader than the silver birch and has browner bark. The leaves and stalks are slightly hairy.

Black Poplar
Populus nigra
Height: 30 metres

The black poplar has a nearly round crown. The leaves are shaped almost like a triangle. Rounded growths, or burrs, often grow on the trunk. It is often planted in industrial regions because it doesn't mind dirty air.

Lombardy Poplar
Populus nigra 'Italica'
Height: 30 metres

This poplar originally came from Lombardy in Italy. You now see it growing along roadsides throughout Europe. Lombardy poplars bear crimson catkins in the spring.

★
Crab Apple
Malus sylvestris

Height: 9 metres

All our favourite apple trees came originally from this bushy tree. Notice that its blossom is paler than that of garden apples. If you taste its small, hard fruits, you will find them very bitter. But they are good for making jelly and wine. Look for clumps of mistletoe on the branches.

Common Pear
Pyrus communis

Height: 15 metres

You may sometimes mix up this tree with the crab apple before the fruit forms. But you can recognize it because its leaves are dark and glossy. Its flowers are snowy white, not pinkish like those of the crab apple.

Cherry Plum
Prunus cerasifera

Height: 8 metres

You often see this small tree in the hedgerows, smothered with white flowers in early March. They come out before the leaves. The branches can be thorny.

★
Holly
Ilex aquifolium

Height: 20 metres

You cannot mistake the holly tree, with its prickly leaves. Notice that they are shiny and dark on top, but paler green and dull underneath. The small white male and female flowers grow on separate trees. You will find berries only on the female trees.

Lobed Leaves

English Oak
Quercus robur
Height: 35 metres

The English oak can live
to be many hundreds of
years old. Notice that the
fruits of this tree, the
acorns, grow on long
stalks. Look for growths,
called galls, on the
leaves.

Scarlet Oak
Quercus coccinea
Height: 26 metres

You cannot mistake this
tree in autumn, because
its leaves turn bright red.
The leaves have clearly
separated lobes and long
stalks. Notice the little
bristles on the lobes. The
acorns are short and fat.

Turkey Oak
Quercus cerris
Height: 38 metres

This originally came from Turkey, but it grows well in northern Europe too. Its leaves are longer and narrower than those of the English oak and are a darker green. Notice that the acorns grow in mossy cups.

Sessile Oak
Quercus petraea
Height: 40 metres

The leaves and acorns of this oak are similar to those of the English oak. So are the flowers, which are like catkins. But one way you can tell them apart is to look at the acorns. On this oak the acorns do not grow on stalks. The word 'sessile' means 'stalkless'.

★

Hawthorn
Cretaegus monogyna
Height: 14 metres

The hawthorn blossoms near May Day and is often called may. The white flowers have a sweet, sickly scent. Notice the long thorns. The red fruit, or haws, provide food for many kinds of birds in winter.

Field Maple
Acer campestre
Height: 26 metres

The field maple has a rounded crown. Its leaves are broad and have three main, rounded lobes. As with all maples, the leaves grow opposite one another on the twigs. The flowers grow in upright spikes. Notice how the pairs of winged seeds form a straight line.

Norway Maple
Acer platanoides

Height: 27 metres

The lobes on the leaves of this maple are pointed. The yellow flowers grow in a rounded head. They come out before the leaves, which are pale green. The winged seeds grow at an angle to each other.

Swedish Whitebeam
Sorbus intermedia

Height: 15 metres

You can often see this small tree planted along the roadsides. In spring you will find it covered with white flower-heads. These are followed by red berries in the autumn. Notice the furry underside of the leaves.

21

Sycamore

Acer pseudoplatanus

Height: 35 metres

The sycamore is the biggest of the maple family of trees. Unlike the other common maples, its flowers grow in catkins. Notice that the stems of its dark green leaves are reddish in colour. Look on the underside of the leaves for tiny, reddish growths, or galls.

White Poplar

Populus alba

Height: 20 metres

The white poplar is a slim tree with light, twisting branches. The leaves grow alternately along the twigs and are wrinkled. Notice that the undersides of the leaves are furry. The flowers and fluffy fruits hang in catkins.

Smooth Japanese Maple
Acer palmatum

Height: 15 metres

This small maple grows very bushy. The five or seven lobes on the leaves are long and pointed. Some varieties have purple leaves.

London Plane
Platanus × hispanica

Height: 30 metres

You find this tree not only in the streets and parks of London, but in cities everywhere. You can usually recognize it by its bark. As the bark gets dirty, it peels off in large flakes, leaving creamy yellow patches. Look for the balls of flowers in the spring and the spiny fruits that follow.

Fig
Ficus carica
Height: 8 metres

In this country you find the bushy fig tree in sheltered places, often against a house wall. The green fruits do not usually ripen here. Notice the very large leaves, which can grow up to 30 cm across.

Tulip Tree
Liriodendron tulipifera
Height: 35 metres

You will probably find this tall tree in parks. It is named after its showy greenish-yellow flowers, which look like tulips.

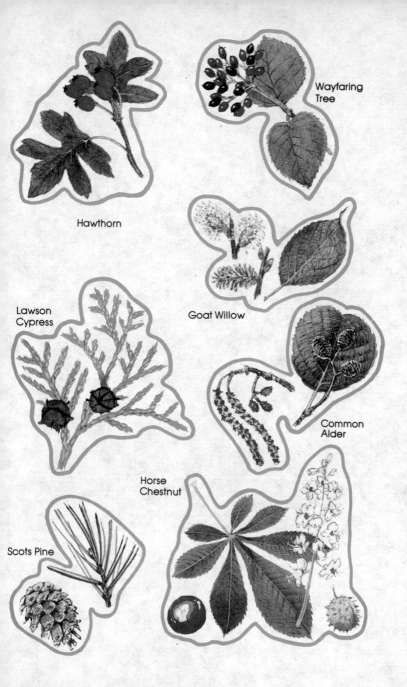

Hawthorn

Wayfaring Tree

Lawson Cypress

Goat Willow

Common Alder

Horse Chestnut

Scots Pine

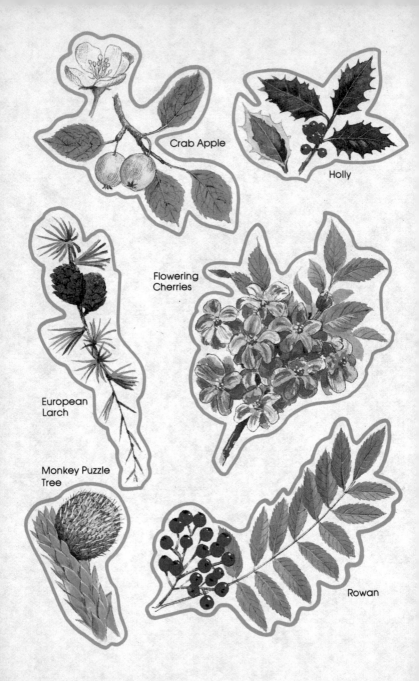

Crab Apple

Holly

Flowering
Cherries

European
Larch

Monkey Puzzle
Tree

Rowan

Maidenhair Tree
Gingko biloba

Height: 30 metres

This tree is found in many parks and gardens. It was one of the earliest trees to appear on the Earth and is unlike any other tree. You can easily recognize it in winter by its spiky-looking branches, and in summer by its fan-shaped leaves.

Wild Service Tree
Sorbus torminalis

Height: 20 metres

This tree is not very common, but it is one of our few native trees. It looks rather like a maple, but its leaves grow alternately along the twigs. It has white flower-heads, which turn into leathery brown berries.

25

Long Leaves

Sweet Chestnut
Castanea sativa

Height: 30 metres

You often find these tall trees planted along avenues in parks and large gardens. Look in the spring for the long, yellow male catkins, and in the autumn for the spiny seed husks.

White Willow
Salix alba

Height: 18 metres

You can recognize this willow by its silvery-green colour. It looks like this because its leaves are covered in silvery hairs, especially underneath.

Crack Willow
Salix fragilis
Height: 24 metres

This willow is named after
the way its branches
easily break when bent.
You often see this tree
pollarded. This means that
the top of the tree is cut
off to allow thin branches
to grow. These are later
cut and used as poles.

Weeping Willow
Salix × chrysocoma or 'Tristis'
Height: 20 metres

The trailing branches give
this tree its name. In spring
notice its golden yellow
branches and young
shoots.

var. 'Kanzan'

var. 'Amanogawa'

★

Flowering Cherries

Prunus serrulata

Many different kinds of flowering cherries have been brought to this country from Japan. They look spectacular in early spring when thick bunches of flowers cover the branches. They come in many shapes and sizes. 'Kanzan' is a popular variety, which has deep pink blossom. It makes quite a large tree. 'Amanogawa' has nearly upright branches and makes a very slender tree. Its blossom is pale pink.

Magnolia

Magnolia × soulangiana

Height: 7 metres

This small tree is a garden favourite. In April look for its huge flowers, which are shaped like cups. They appear before the leaves.

Almond

Prunus dulcis

Height: 9 metres

You often see almond trees planted by the roadside. When they blossom, you know that spring is on the way. Notice that the pink flowers come out before the leaves. The green fruit holds a single oval nut, which has a pitted surface.

Spindle
Euonymus europaeus
Height: 6 metres

The spindle is an open little tree with few branches. It has small, white flowers in spring. It carries dull, pink fruits in autumn, when the leaves turn dark red. The hard wood of the tree was once used to make spindles for spinning.

Holm Oak
Quercus ilex
Height: 27 metres

You can easily recognize this oak in winter, because it keeps its dark leaves—it is evergreen. Notice that the undersides of the leaves are white and slightly furry.

Bird Cherry
Prunus padus
Height: 9 metres

This cherry grows well in the north and is often found near streams. The white flowers grow in long spikes and have a strong scent like almonds. The cherries grow on the spikes and turn black when ripe.

Wild Cherry
Prunus avium
Height: 12 metres

You often find this tree in beech woods. It is sometimes grown for its timber. It is covered in white blossom in spring. The cherries turn reddish-yellow in autumn.

31

Compound Leaves

✶ Horse Chestnut
Aesculus hippocastanum

Height: 35 metres

You can easily recognize
this large tree because of
its hand-shaped leaves.
These have up to seven
leaflets. In spring the tree
carries large spikes of
white flowers, and in
autumn, spiny fruits. When
the fruits fall, they split
open and let out the shiny
brown seeds, or conkers.

✶

Rowan (opposite)
Sorbus aucuparia

Height: 20 metres

The rowan is also called
the mountain ash,
because it can often be
found growing high up.
It is a graceful tree, with
open branches.

Laburnum
Laburnum anagyroides

Height: 7 metres

This is a small tree with arching branches, often found in gardens. It produces dangling clusters of bright yellow flowers in spring. These turn into pods containing black seeds. Both flowers and seeds are **poisonous**.

Ash

Fraxinus excelsior

Height: 40 metres

The ash is a tall tree, with a straight trunk. You can recognize it at any time of the year by its fat, black buds. The tiny, purple flowers come out before the leaves. The seeds that form have long wings and hang in bunches.

Elder

Sambucus nigra

Height: 9 metres

This bushy tree provides a feast for birds in the autumn, with its bunches of purple-black berries. Look for its flat, white flower-heads in the hedgerows in spring.

Walnut
Juglans regia
Height: 30 metres

The walnut tree has a broad, rounded crown. The familiar crinkled walnut ripens inside a green fruit. Look in the spring for the male catkins and tiny, upright, female flowers.

Robinia
Robinia pseudoacacia
Height: 25 metres

This tree is also called the false acacia or locust tree. You can recognize it by its leaflets. They are rounded and have a small spine on the end. The white flowers hang in bunches. They change into brown pods, which contain black seeds.

35

Needle-Like Leaves

★ **European Larch**
Larix decidua
Height: 38 metres

Larches are the only conifers that are not evergreen. The European larch is a graceful tree with curving branches. Its needles are light green and grow in rosettes.

Winter

Monterey Pine
Pinus radiata

Stone Pine
Pinus pinea

Bhutan Pine
Pinus wallichiana

Corsican Pine
Pinus nigra maritima

Height: 35 metres

The Corsican pine has quite a narrow shape. The needles are long and grow in pairs. The bark is dark grey.

★
Scots Pine
Pinus sylvestris

Height: 36 metres

You find this pine not only in Scotland, but everywhere in Britain. It is an important timber tree. Old trees have a broad crown, but few branches lower down. The bluish-grey needles are quite short and grow in pairs, and the bark is reddish-brown.

Blue Spruce
Picea pungens 'Glauca'
Height: 24 metres

This spruce has bluish needles, which grow thickly all around the branches. It is narrower than the Norway spruce. It is often called the Colorado spruce after the place it first came from.

Norway Spruce
Picea abies
Height: 40 metres

We know this better as the Christmas tree. Notice that the short needles grow all round the branches. In May look for the pinkish female flowers and yellow male flowers.

Sitka Spruce
Picea sitchensis
Height: 46 metres

The Sitka spruce is now one of our commonest timber trees. It is the tallest of the spruces. The needles are bluish-green. You can recognize this spruce best by its smooth bark, which peels off in round patches.

Cedar of Lebanon
Cedrus libani
Height: 35 metres

You can always recognize this magnificent tree by its shape The foliage grows in flat layers at various levels up the tree, and forms a very broad crown. Notice that the dark green needles grow in rosettes. Look for the spike left on the branches when the cones break up and shed their seeds.

Common Juniper
Juniperus communis
Height: 6 metres

You often find the juniper growing in beech woods, especially in chalky soils. Notice that the spiky leaves grow in sets of three along the branches. Look for the purple fruits.

Common Yew
Taxus baccata
Height: 15 metres

Yews grow into large, rounded trees. You often see them in churchyards and also growing wild. Birds love the sticky, red berries. The leaves and berries are **poisonous**.

Western Hemlock
Tsuga heterophylla

Height: 35 metres

The flat needles of this timber tree are green on top and white underneath. You can recognize the tree from the way its shoots and branches droop down at the ends. Notice how small the cones are.

Monkey Puzzle Tree
Araucaria araucana

Height: 24 metres

This tree is easy to recognize. Its branches are covered with triangular leaves, which have very sharp spines. It is also called the Chile pine, because it comes from Chile in South America.

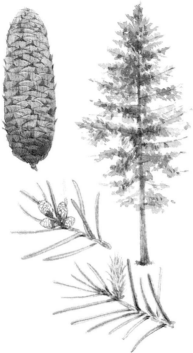

Common Silver Fir
Abies alba
Height: 45 metres

This tall tree has open branches. The needles are flat, and there are 'partings' between them on the twigs. The needles are green above and silvery underneath. The female flowers grow on top, and the male flowers underneath.

Grand Fir
Abies grandis
Height: 55 metres

This is similar to the silver fir, but has thicker foliage, and the flat needles are shinier. The cones of the silver and grand firs are different too, but are usually out of sight at the top of the tree.

Douglas Fir
Pseudotsuga menziesii
Height: 55 metres

You can find this very tall tree in parks and also in timber forests. The flat needles have two white stripes underneath. The scaly cones hang down from the branches.

Noble Fir
Abies procera
Height: 45 metres

You can easily recognize this fir by its branches, which stick straight out in layers. The flat needles are bluish-green. They grow all around the twigs and usually curve upwards. Look for the spikes left on the branches when the cones break up.

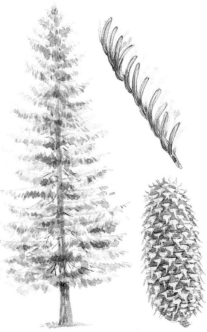

Scaly Leaves

★ Lawson Cypress
Chamaecyparis lawsoniana
Height: 36 metres

You see the Lawson cypress in gardens everywhere. There are many different varieties, which all have different shapes. Some common ones are pictured opposite. The tallest is the standard tree (left). Notice the way the shoot at the top of the tree droops. You will find many of the small cones all over the tree.

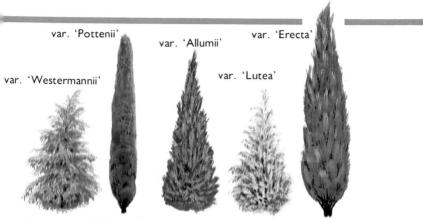

var. 'Pottenii'

var. 'Allumii'

var. 'Erecta'

var. 'Westermannii'

var. 'Lutea'

Common varieties of Lawson cypress

Leyland Cypress

x *Cupressocyparis leylandii*

Height: 30 metres

This is another very popular garden tree, which is often clipped to form a hedge. It grows much faster than the other conifers. The leaves are a brighter green than those of the Lawson cypress. Another good way of telling these cypresses apart is by looking at the flowers. On the Leyland cypress you can hardly see the green female flowers, and the male flowers are yellow. You will find few cones.

45

Western Red Cedar
Thuja plicata

Height: 25 metres

The western red cedar looks much like the Lawson and Leyland cypresses, but there are a few differences. Its leaves are broader, and the growing shoot at the top of the tree is upright, not drooping. Also, the cones are barrel-shaped.

Monterey Cypress
Cupressus macrocarpa

Height: 30 metres

This is often planted in gardens near the seaside, because it is not damaged by salty winds. The scaly leaves are tiny and the cones are large and round. The bark is yellowish-brown.

Wellingtonia
Sequoiadendron giganteum
Height: 46 metres

This huge tree is named after the Duke of Wellington. It is also called the giant sequoia after its Latin name. Notice the way the branches curve down and then up at the ends.

Chinese Juniper
Juniperis virginiana
Height: 18 metres

This attractive, slim tree is planted widely in gardens. In the autumn it is covered with small blue-green fruits, which turn purple after two years. Notice the way the bark peels off in long strips.

Index